# Map Symbols and Scales

BY SAMANTHA S. BELL

**The Child's World**
childsworld.com

Published by The Child's World®
1980 Lookout Drive • Mankato, MN 56003-1705
800-599-READ • www.childsworld.com

Photographs ©: Ales Krivec/Shutterstock Images,
cover (background), 1; Shutterstock Images, cover
(foreground), 6, 9; Mr. Aekalak Chimacharoen/
Shutterstock Images, 5; iStockphoto, 10; Nadya
Eugene/Shutterstock Images, 13; James Mattil/
Shutterstock Images, 14; Fang Xia Nuo/
iStockphoto, 17; Red Line Editorial, 19

ISBN Hardcover: 9781503827691
ISBN Paperback: 9781622434503
LCCN: 2018944818

Printed in the United States of America
PA02397

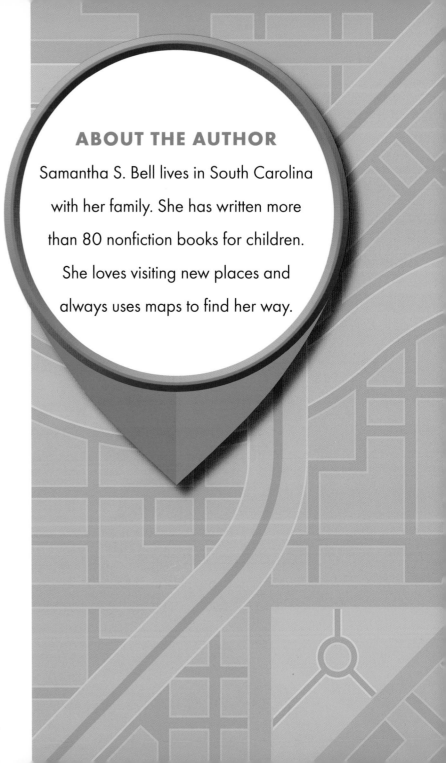

## ABOUT THE AUTHOR

Samantha S. Bell lives in South Carolina with her family. She has written more than 80 nonfiction books for children. She loves visiting new places and always uses maps to find her way.

# TABLE OF CONTENTS

# CHAPTER ONE

# Reading Maps

You are moving to a new town with your family. You have never been there before. Your family uses a map to help get there. After you move, you use maps to find your way around the area. Neighborhood maps can show schools and churches. Park maps show playgrounds, trails, and picnic areas.

Maps can show many different kinds of places.

5

We can use maps while hiking to find out how far we need to go.

When you look at a map, you might see a lot of lines or little pictures called **icons**. There are also **symbols** on a map. Each symbol **represents** something in the area.

Most maps also have a **scale**. The scale tells us about **distance**. Scales are used to show how far apart things are on Earth compared to the map.

Maps show us where to go. With symbols and scales, they tell us about the things around us, too.

# CHAPTER TWO

# Types of Symbols

The symbols on a map show important **features** people might need to know. Some symbols are the same on most maps. Lines are used for roads and rivers. Dots or stars show where cities are located.

Maps have symbols that make them easy to use.

Maps show the location of important places, such as airports.

Sometimes maps use icons for symbols. An airplane can represent an airport. A tree might represent a park.

Some symbols are point symbols. Point symbols show exactly where something is on the map. Dots and stars are point symbols. Icons are point symbols, too.

Some symbols are lines. They may be used to show a **boundary** between countries or states.

Lines are often used when a feature is long. Roads are usually drawn as black lines. Rivers are usually drawn as blue lines.

The lines on a map might represent roads.

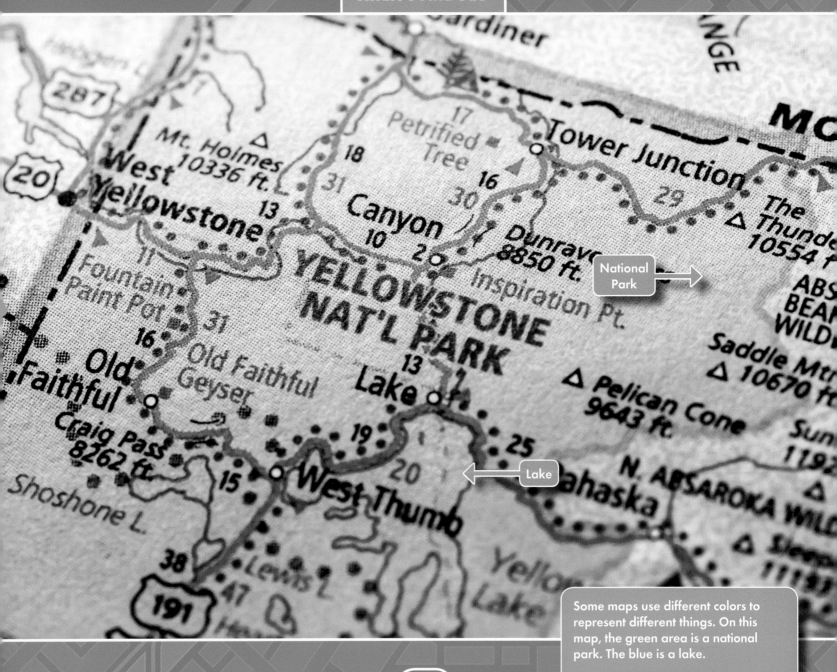

National Park

Lake

Some maps use different colors to represent different things. On this map, the green area is a national park. The blue is a lake.

Sometimes certain areas on a map are shaded with color. The color is called an area symbol. Green usually represents forests. Tan represents deserts. Blue represents lakes or oceans. States and countries can be different colors, too.

Most maps have a key, or legend. The key tells what each symbol means. The symbols and the key help you find what is on the map.

# CHAPTER THREE

# Types of Scales

Some scales tell us how far it is from one place to another. Others tell us how big something is.

A verbal scale shows two numbers on either side of an equal sign. The first number is a measurement on the map. The second number is the distance on Earth. The numbers help us figure out how far apart things are. For example, it might say 1 inch = 1 **mile**. This means 1 inch on the map is equal to 1 mile on Earth.

You can use a scale to find out how far away something is.

Some scales are called bar scales. A bar scale looks like a ruler. Bar scales are like verbal scales. They show how a measurement on the map compares to the distance on Earth.

Some scales are called RF scales. An RF scale looks like a **fraction** or a **ratio**. It tells us how big the real area is. For example, the RF scale might say 1/1,000 or 1:1,000. This means that the real area is 1,000 times bigger than the area on the map.

People use maps to find out about different places. Symbols and scales help them understand the maps.

# SCALE

0                          10

MILES

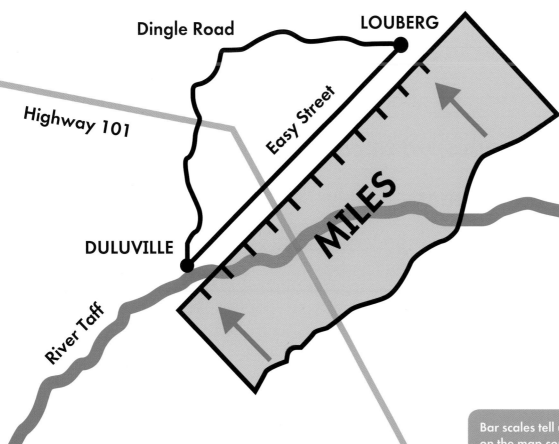

Dingle Road

LOUBERG

Highway 101

Easy Street

DULUVILLE

MILES

River Taff

Bar scales tell us how the distance on the map compares to the distance on Earth.

# Do You Know?

**Q:** What color usually represents oceans on a map?

**A:** Blue

**Q:** On a map, what can a long line represent?

**A:** A road or river

**Q:** What does a map scale tell us?

**A:** It tells us how the distance on a map compares to the distance on Earth.

**Q:** Can you think of icons you might see on a map of your city?

**Q:** When would you need to use a map legend?

**Q:** Have you ever used a map scale?

# Glossary

**boundary** (BOWN-duh-ree) A boundary is a dividing line that shows the end or limit of something. A map can show the boundary between two countries.

**distance** (DISS-tuhnss) Distance is the amount of space between two points. Scales help us understand distance on maps.

**features** (FEE-churz) Features are parts or details that stand out. Mountains are natural features.

**fraction** (FRAK-shuhn) A fraction is a part of something whole. An RF scale shows a fraction.

**icons** (EYE-konz) Icons are pictures used to illustrate something. Trees could be icons that represent a forest.

**mile** (MILE) A mile is a unit of measure that equals 5,280 feet (approximately 1,609 meters). On some maps, one inch on the map can equal one mile on Earth.

**ratio** (RAY-shee-oh) A ratio shows the relationship in quantity, amount, or size between two things. The ratio on a map can show how far things are from each other on Earth.

**represents** (rep-ri-ZENTZ) Represents means to serve as a sign for something else. Sometimes a line on a map represents a river.

**scale** (SKALE) A scale is a measurement of distance on a map. A scale can show how far two places are from each other on a map.

**symbols** (SIM-buhlz) Symbols are designs that represent something else. Maps use symbols to show features on maps.

# To Learn More

### BOOKS

Olien, Rebecca. *Map Keys*. New York, NY: Children's Press, 2013.

Quinlan, Julia. *Keys, Legends, and Symbols in Maps*.
New York, NY: Powerkids Press, 2012.

Shea, Therese. *Reading Map Keys*. New York,
NY: Gareth Stevens Publishing, 2015.

Wade, Mary Dodson. *Map Scales*. New York, NY: Children's Press, 2013.

### WEB SITES

Visit our Web site for links about map symbols and scales:
**childsworld.com/links**

*Note to Parents, Teachers, and Librarians: We routinely verify our Web links to make sure they are safe and active sites. So encourage your readers to check them out!*

# Index